HOME SERIES

HOME SERIES
COMPACT SPACES

BETA-PLUS

CONTENTS

P. 4-5
The modestly sized living room
in a holiday home decorated by
Claudine Vasseur. The use of
white as the base colour makes
the room very light.

P. 6
For more space in this narrow
hallway, AIDarchitects found a
clever, aesthetic solution for the
oak staircase by revisiting the
principle of "staggered stairs"
or "monk's stairs".

INTRODUCTION

O ften a synonym for small areas, compact spaces are generally quite open, multifunctional places.

However, having a visual approach to the space from the very beginning is essential for deciding on layout and optimising space. Successful compact spaces are often areas where movement is fluid and there is no shortage of sensible, discreet storage options.

A carefully considered layout is essential to make the most of every last centimetre and for getting every function to coexist in a compact space where everything still needs to be there.

To create the illusion of a larger space, there are certain tried and tested tactics to focus on. Special attention should be paid to plays on luminosity, perspectives, reflections, movement between rooms, and lighting. For example, mid-height partition furniture maintains intimacy, provides definition to individual areas and structures the space, at the same time as preserving freedom of movement and allowing the gaze to move through the area unhindered.

The method used often consists of creating order for amplification and erasing for preservation. Understatedness is well-suited to compact spaces: clean, light lines bring out the volume of space. An accumulation of various pieces of furniture simply placed against the walls, ceiling lights and shimmering materials can rapidly smother a room, absorb the light and make the room shrink from a visual point of view. A choice of furniture in correct proportions, adapted to the size of the room, is naturally an excellent way of freeing up maximum space. A choice of light colours and cold shading is often preferable: even if they do not have the same character, they have the advantage of increasing space.

In the examples in this book, you will find solutions and effective tips for making the most of your space.

P. 8
Optimal use of space in this bathroom designed by designer and architect Gérard Faivre.

P. 10-11
Bulthaup kitchen in a holiday home in Ramatuelle, created by architect Mouniguet and designed by Christel De Vos (De Vos Projects) and Nathalie Mousny. Botticino stone work surfaces and stools designed by Bataille + ibens. Dining room chairs by Meridiani.

IN SEARCH

OF OPENNESS AND SPACE

I n a building built in the 1930s, located on Avenue de Lowendal in Paris, architect Antonio Virga has renovated an apartment that previously had numerous small rooms and turned it into a new ensemble full of openness and space.

The number of doors is kept to a bare minimum, and most of them have been replaced by pivoting doors, where they are unavoidable.

The key objective: making the feeling of closed off, segregated spaces fade in order to give a strong identity to the apartment as a whole and bring all the rooms together.

For example, the kitchen – equipped with a glass wall to allow daylight to enter – is now entirely open to the entrance hall.

The vast combined living and dining room is entirely designed with its length in mind, with a long concrete bench to establish a link between the two functions.

Here, Antonio Virga has created the full project to measure, including integrating the furniture.
The old oak floorboards laid in the entrance hall extend into the living room adjoining the dining room.
Moroccan rug. Maxalto ceiling lights.

Note...

> The built-in bookcase. Although it is not very deep (15 cm are enough), it provides an unusual storage solution for books and CDs.

> The perspective accentuated by the two suspended lamps and the painting at the vanishing point at the end creates a very decorative entrance.

Remember...

> Despite the narrow nature of the living room, the space is airy. The secret to this lightness lies in the simplicity of the decoration: no curtains, little carpeting, and no massive suspended light fitting, just discreet lamps.

> The choice of furniture in proportion to suit the place: a narrow dining room table and no low table, as this has been replaced by a concrete bench that runs the length of the wall.

The many small rooms have been brought together to form a whole. The sofa was made to measure. The chairs around the table are from Padova, and the bench is cast concrete. Lighting from Flos and LucePlan.

The kitchen walls are made of steel and glass. The work surfaces are in stainless steel, natural stone and Corian, while the high wall cupboards are in brushed, tinted oak. The lighting in this room is also from Flos (Glo-Ball model). Resin floor.

Design Ideas

> The same minimalist aesthetic desire applies to the kitchen: discreet, white furniture without handles that blends into the walls and no curtains.

> A resin floor is an alternative to a concrete floor, and is a highly contemporary look that increases space due to the lack of joins.

Warm, earthy colours contrast with the white painted walls. The red rug is Moroccan and the cushions are from Mali.

The bathroom floor is in concrete. The washbasins were made to measure based on designs by architect Virga. The drawers and cupboards are in brushed, tinted oak.

A FRIENDLY LITTLE APARTMENT

This friendly apartment by the sea was designed by C&C Designburo. Interior architect Martine Cammaert focused on the harmony of the surroundings and materials throughout the apartment. To increase the space from a visual point of view, very light shades and natural materials were chosen. The paintings were commissioned from Kordekor.

The very rational arrangement of the living room and numerous discreet storage solutions allow space to be freed up.

The view from the kitchen provides direct contact with the living room.

The floor and high, made to measure cupboards are in bleached oak.

Note...

> The sliding partition on the bar: a clever way to completely conceal the kitchen.

> The optimisation of space: none is wasted, due to the two shallow cupboards either side of the bar for maximum storage.

The bar work surface and the kitchen walls have been covered in natural Pietra Piasentina stone by the company Van den Weghe.

A unity of materials, including in the bathroom: as in the kitchen, natural Pietra Piasentina stone is also used here (a Van den Weghe creation, following a project by C&C Designburo).

Design Ideas

> The mirror hung beside the sink as well as in front increases a sense of space and avoids a feeling of isolation.

THE CHARM OF

AN ATMOSPHERIC OUTBUILDING

E nglish Heritage Buildings started out in the Benelux countries 12 years ago, designing and building carports and garages in oak.

Since then, the company has considerably expanded its skill set. Its list of references now includes pool houses, guesthouses, home offices and annexes.

The house shown in this section dates from the 1980s. It is located in an idyllic spot on a hill in Grez-Doiceau (Walloon Brabant).

English Heritage Buildings was commissioned to add a huge living room, a TV room and a large bedroom to an existing house.

The company had carte blanche. With a view to preserving the aesthetics, different levels were created between the new living room and the TV room.

Consequently, the whole ensemble seems smaller from the outside, which makes it all more welcoming.

Following an artisanal tradition dating back centuries, the whole of the oak structure was assembled using mortise and tenon joints.

The walls and ceiling of the TV room were painted dark grey.
Only the oak beams were left untreated in order to reinforce the authenticity of the place.
The large screen is built into the last oak beam and rolls out in front of the cabinet as needed.

The new living room has been completely painted white in order to further highlight the beautiful antiques.

Large patio doors offer an impressive view of the surrounding hills.

Note...

> In spite of all the eclectic accessories, the space is lightened by the lack of curtains and rugs. The eye is drawn to the house unhindered.

> To create more visual distance, the ceiling beams are painted white while the others have kept their natural shade and original style.

The oak structure is fully assembled with mortise and tenon joints.

Note...

> The different levels provide the space with rhythm and structure. They can also increase it by creating new perspectives.

BACK TO THE SOURCE

IN BLACK AND WHITE

T he FilipTackdesignoffice specialises in architecture, interior design and object design.

This 1920s apartment has undergone a profound transformation in order to meet modern comfort needs and fulfil a variety of functions. Interior designer Filip Tack created a feeling of space and favoured the selection of natural materials. The design goes back to basics through a subtle play on the spaces and walls, and the floors are raised to different levels.

The whole ensemble now has a contemporary, clean style.

A long corridor at the entrance connects the apartment to the stairwell. As the view at the back was not very important to the owners, a woven leather drape was placed in front of the windows. The daylight is therefore filtered and distributed diffusely. At the end of the corridor, the emphasis is on the wash hand basin.

P.41-45
The furniture, accessories, paintings and drapes were chosen in consultation between the owners, Rouge Safran and FilipTackdesignoffice.
The central unit in the kitchen is made of stainless steel. The cupboard, in brushed anthracite oak, is graphically inspired. The hinged joints are door handles, the recess opens electronically. The TV wall and bookcase consist of a separate cupboard made to measure in matt sanded oak, with an ultra-gloss white paint finish. All the technical installations have been carefully built in.

Note...

> A carefully thought-out, sensibly divided living room that combines three functions in a fairly restricted space. The kitchen, dining room and living room are side by side, thanks to subtly suggested partitions. The bar provides definition to a very discreet kitchen, the large suspended lamp marks the dining area, and the sofa, which backs on to the dining area, creates the partition with the TV corner.

> Highly discreet, chic storage: the walls at the back of the kitchen mask some of the domestic appliances and make the kitchen invisible.

The desk with built-in drawer has
been painted matt white.

All the furniture in the master bedroom is made to measure. Hästens bed.

In the bathrooms, the floors, panelling and washbasins were also made to measure based on a design by FilipTackdesignoffice, in polished Gris Sau. Chrome taps. In the toilets, the washbasin and the mirror were made to measure based on a personal design. Natural stone: Gris Sau. The mirror frame is made of Macassar wood.

CHANGE IN STYLE

wners who embark on renovation works rightly expect a lot from their designers.

These desires can often be expressed in a single sentence: provide us with a design, within a reasonable deadline and at a reasonable price, where high-quality materials are used and the personality of the occupants is reflected, for a place where we can feel at home. Today's designer is therefore above all someone who develops and combines styles. Someone who is multi-skilled enough to move easily from one design to another.

Construmax is a company that happily meets these demands and does everything it can to guide the customer through the mysteries of the construction process.
The designs presented in this section illustrate that approach.

This kitchen, in a gabled suburban house, radiates rustic charm thanks to the materials used. Oak was chosen for the cupboard doors, combined with blue stone work surfaces and a terracotta floor in various colours.

Modern entrepreneurs are often inspired by the cross-pollination that constantly occurs between the designs produced. For this reason, different styles can often be mixed easily in a single residential building at the request of its inhabitants.
This house is a striking example of such a mix of styles. Its inhabitants wanted quite modern, understated lines, but without sacrificing the warmth of a rustic environment.

Note...

> The full-length glass door: a way of visually freeing up space.

> The multi-function unit, doubling as a fireplace and TV corner, which serves as a partial partition with the dining room section, maintaining the softness of the room.

In the same house, a modern bathroom without too many embellishments was resolutely chosen. Here, the straight lines are only interrupted by the rounded shapes of the sinks, by the warmth of the atmospheric lighting and by the light-hearted lettering on the shower wall ('shower' in French).

WARM MINIMALISM

In this project, the owner gave carte blanche to Nicolaas Van Ransbeeck to design her attic apartment.

In consultation with the client, Van Ransbeeck took on the design and creation of the kitchen, bathroom, inside doors, lighting, paintwork, etc.

A complete project coordinated from A to Z by the interior designer's office.

The space is organised rationally and the storage solutions were studied in detail: partitions serve as cupboards, while other storage is hidden in the fireplace surround.

The living room includes a concealed light vault containing Kreon moveable bulbs.
Metal glazed sliding doors and a completely open kitchen.
Le Corbusier white club armchair.

Design ideas

> The striped wall creates both a decorative look and depth.

> A single large corner sofa rather than several chairs to free up space and create a contemporary style.

The plasma screen lift was designed and created by Van Ransbeeck: a truly unique piece, with vertical movement of 160 cm.

Painting by Anton Heyboer.

Cabinets made to measure in 1 cm thick brushed stainless steel, with built-in mirrors and lighting.
All the natural stonework used in this bathroom is Portuguese Branco de Mos marble. For the showers, small mosaics in Nero Marquina marble and zelliges.
The wood chosen for the sink and bath cladding is a wenge-tinted French oak.

AN OASIS

OF CALM AND LIGHTNESS

Obumex produced the interior design of a minimalist apartment for a contemporary art collector.

In spite of a limited area, Xavier Gadeyne, senior interior designer at Obumex, succeeded – in collaboration with the client – in transforming this coastal apartment into an oasis of calm.

By using white throughout, in combination with austere lines, this 90 m2 apartment appears to be much more spacious than it actually is.

The choice of furniture is also vital for the perception of this feeling of space. Here again, all the pieces of furniture have a clean, subtle, light design, so that the space can flow.

The corner sofa and the white lacquered coffee table were selected from the Charles collection by B&B Italia. The understated black leather armchair stands on a sandy-coloured rug made from a mix of cloth and wool.

The chrome finish, devised by Jeppe Hein, is also present in the details of the furniture and gives the space a lively, dynamic character.

P.70-71
The white lacquered Athos table (B&B Italia) is placed at the end of the corner sofa. It can therefore be used as a dining table or console table.

A made to measure sink and an electronic tap have been cunningly built into the one-piece white-lacquered kitchen block. This centrally positioned block also includes a white Corian board.

A work by the German artist Anselm Reyle hangs on the long white wall, producing a confident contrast.

Note...

> The graphical, discreet effect for the rows of spotlights on the ceiling.

> A small, discreet yet highly functional kitchen thanks to an optimal central block with a clean-lined design.

> The coherence and harmony of the furniture form a sure foundation for increasing the space. Disparate elements reduce the visual sense of space.

Note...

> The light that comes in through the sliding doors in acid-etched glass and the longitudinal orientation of the flooring give the whole ensemble a genuinely striking feeling of depth.

> The lateral arrangement of the lighting in the floor and the ceiling-height doors enlarge the hall from a visual point of view.

A glass sliding door separates the main bedroom from the open dressing room. Charles bed (B&B Italia).

The epoxy resin floor continues seamlessly into the shower.
The walls of this space and the sink unit are covered in white lacquered glass panels.

A PARISIAN PIED-À-TERRE

Éric Gizard's office (EGA) produced the interior of this apartment in Paris's 16th arrondissement.

The 90 m² area was studied, considered and designed to perfectly match the American lifestyle of the owners.

Creation of two bedrooms, two bathrooms and a kitchen, with optimal integration of dressing rooms and extensive storage: to meet these requirements, Éric Gizard carried out comprehensive work on flow and movement in this new, restructured space.

The reassuring comfort of the Knoll furniture invites relaxation in an atmosphere where technology has not been forgotten: a thorough study was performed on the lights and home automation of sound and images in all the spaces.

Design ideas

> The painted storage solutions bring gloss and depth.

> The large mirror reflects the space and provides light.

> A limited range of colours: white and brown. The furniture (bookcase, dining room table) merge with the floor and walls.

A selection of elegant, delicate materials: dark wood contrasts with the engraved glass partitions by Guillaume Saalburg (Techniques Transparentes), while the fawn colour of the leather complements the tobacco brown curtains.

Note...

> An optimised kitchen made to measure. It is based around the domestic appliances and provides maximum storage. The refrigerator and oven are discreetly built into recesses; every last centimetre is used to the full.

Decoration idea

> An effective optical illusion for hiding storage: the base of the wall extends into cupboards that then become invisible.

The cashmere bedcovers put the finishing touch on the delicacy of the ensemble.
Simply chic: two words that encapsulate the design of this Parisian pied-à-terre.

RESTRUCTURING

A DUPLEX APARTMENT

P resented with a duplex apartment that no longer had any feature worthy of interest, architect Antonio Virga decided to completely restructure its two floors.

The guiding principle was to create continuity between the rooms without the use of a corridor to avoid wasting any place. The architect devised double doors that can remain open or provide a partition between two spaces. The day apartments are located on the ground floor while the night apartments are on the first floor.

The new staircase, lit by a light well, provides a linking point between the two levels.

The oak floor has been tinted black. The doors and stair treads have been treated in the same way.

Note...

> A highly uncluttered space using low furniture to allow the gaze to move freely.

> The 'floating' staircase is a strong graphic element as a sculpture, as well as taking up the minimum of space.

> (see next page) Clever, elegant partition furniture to separate the living room from the kitchen/dining room.

P.92-95

The table was made to measure. Work surface in natural stone, furniture in satin-finished stainless steel. Maxalto lighting. Behind, two Maxalto sofas, a Fat-Fat footstool from B&B Italia, a concrete bench and a Glo-Ball light from Flos.

The bed and footrest are from Maxalto.

The bathroom floor and the bath are made of natural Lecce stone. The sinks are in Pietra Serena.

The made-to-measure furniture in the library/office space is made of natural oak.

TRANSFORMING

AN OLD WORKSHOP INTO A CONTEMPORARY HOUSE

T he Julie Brion et Tanguy Leclercq AD architect's practice completely transformed an old workshop behind a house in a lively urban area into a little house. The whole ensemble now has a very understated, clean-lined character: soft minimalism with warm tones.

The practice made an in-depth study of the light and light fittings that give the space an unusual dimension.

Julie Brion and Tanguy Leclercq designed a 16m long unit covered with a concrete beam to unite the various successive spaces that form the living room, dining room and kitchen. The fireplace also serves as a projection wall thanks to the special paint it is covered with.

The natural light marks the join between the extension and the existing building.

P.104-105
The entrance is marked by a forced circulation point created by the erection of a low wall complex with a double-function cloakroom/bookcase block designed by Julie Brion and Tanguy Leclercq.
This set-up creates a visual opening and access for light from the side.

The living room furniture beam extends into the kitchen and uses the difference in level to become the kitchen work surface.

Note...

> The strip lights installed all the way along the low storage, which provide soft light and decorate the wall.

> A feeling of space accentuated by the perspectives and plays on levels.

> Light colours that reflect the light.

View from the kitchen into the open space that forms the dining room and the living room.

Decoration idea

> In spite of its small size, the bedroom is an interesting room. The four-poster bed alone personalises the décor.

The aggregate floor of the shower room is continuous for maximum comfort of movement. The architects opted for a translucent glass partition to bring light into the bathrooms.

The stairwell is lit with a pair of light-filled hollows that accentuate its verticality.

The bathroom is bathed in light thanks to a translucent floor-to-ceiling glass partition.

HOME SERIES

Volume 20 : COMPACT SPACES

The reports in this book are selected from the Beta-Plus collection of home-design books: www.betaplus.com
They have been compiled in a special series by Le Figaro in French language: Ma Déco

Copyright © 2009 Beta-Plus Publishing / Le Figaro
Originally published in French language

PUBLISHER
Beta-Plus Publishing
Termuninck 3
B – 7850 Enghien
Belgium
www.betaplus.com
info@betaplus.com

TEXT
Alexandra Druesne

PHOTOGRAPHY
Jo Pauwels

DESIGN
Polydem - Nathalie Binart

TRANSLATIONS
Txt-Ibis

ISBN: 978-90-8944-051-8

Printed in China